CW00348048

HUMPHREY THE HIPPO

CHRIS RIDDELL

GRAFTON BOOKS
A Division of the Collins Publishing Group

LONDON GLASGOW
TORONTO SYDNEY AUCKLAND

'Tomorrow's my birthday,' said Humphrey the Hippo. 'And the postman hasn't brought me any presents or cards yet. It's boring.'

'You won't be bored tomorrow,' promised his best friend Bird. But more than that he would not say.

The next day, early in the morning, Bird led Humphrey down to see his birthday present – a shiny red motorbike.

'Happy Birthday!' said Bird.

'Let's go for a ride!' Humphrey cried.

'Not in your pyjamas and dressing gown!'
said Bird.

So Humphrey and Bird put on their new
motorcycling outfits.

'Do I have to wear this hat?' asked Humphrey.

'Of course,' said Bird. 'You've never seen a hippo on a bike without one, have you?'

Bird read out the instructions from a book. 'Kick the starter pedal,' he said – and began to cough, as a cloud of smoke blew out at him.

Pop, pop, pop went the motorbike. And someone called, 'Go away, you'll wake the baby!'

So off they went. 'Look where you're going!' cried Bird.

Humphrey took no notice.

'Watch out!' cried Bird as they swerved round the milkman.

'You made him drop your birthday cards,' said Bird as they dodged past the postman.

'Never mind, this is fun!' yelled Humphrey.

Soon they were out in the country. They were looking for a place to have a picnic

when BANG one of the tyres got a
puncture.

So they stopped to mend the puncture and ate their picnic there and then.

'Lovely view,' said Bird.

'Beastly bike,' grumbled Humphrey.

Humphrey was so cross he went really fast.

'Slow down! Look where you're going!' Bird cried.

'Why should I when you've got your eyes covered up?' Humphrey shouted.

Oh no! Off the road and into a pond they went.

Splash! went Humphrey and Bird.

Splutter! Splutter! went the shiny red
motorbike.

But Humphrey didn't mind.

'Mud, mud, glorious mud,' he crooned.

Then out they climbed and the farmer who owned the pond gave them a lift home on his tractor.

'Can I have a tractor for my next birthday?' asked Humphrey.

'We'll see,' said Bird.

For Jo

Grafton Books
A Division of the Collins Publishing Group
8 Grafton Street, London W1X 3LA

Published by Grafton Books 1986
Copyright © Chris Riddell 1986

British Library Cataloguing in Publication Data
Riddell, Chris
Humphrey the hippo.
I. Title
823'.914[J]   PZ7

ISBN 0-246-12964-6

Printed in Belgium by
Henri Proost

All rights reserved. No part of this publication
may be reproduced, stored in a retrieval system, or
transmitted, in any form or by any means, electronic,
mechanical, photocopying, recording or otherwise,
without prior permission of the publishers.

PRINTED IN BELGIUM BY

proost
INTERNATIONAL BOOK PRODUCTION